The Montreal Canadiens

Hockey Champions

Bob Italia

Published by Abdo & Daughters, 4940 Viking Drive, Suite 622, Edina, Minnesota 55435.

Library bound edition distributed by Rockbottom Books, Pentagon Tower, P.O. Box 36036, Minneapolis, Minnesota 55435. International copyrights reserved in all countries. No part of this book may be reproduced in any form without written permission from the publisher. Printed in the United States.

Cover Photo By: Doug MacLellan/Hockey Hall of Fame
Interior Photos by: Doug MacLellan/Hockey Hall of Fame: pgs. 4, 5, 7, 8, 11, 12, 14,
16, 20, 26, 28-30
Allsport Photo, Inc.: pgs. 10, 18, 21, 23, 25

Edited By: Rosemary Wallner

LIBRARY OF CONGRESS CATALOGING-IN-PUBLICATION DATA

Italia, Robert, 1955-
        The Montreal Canadiens / by Robert Italia.
                p.   cm. -- (The Year in Sports)
        Includes bibliographical references and glossary.
        ISBN 1-56239-240-9
        1. Montreal Canadiens (Hockey team) -- Juvenile literature.
        I. Title. II. Series: The Year in Sports (Edina, Minn.).
        GV848.M6I85 1993
        796.962'64'0971427--dc20   93-30672
                                                        CIP
                                                        AC

Contents

Not Enough Offense 4

Slow Start 5

The Shake-Up 5

The Offense Kicks-In High Gear 6

Streaking Along 6

Sweet Revenge 6

Savvy Savard 6

The Comeback Kids 7

Skrudland Skates 7

An Offensive Defense 8

Damphousse Arrives 9

The Veterans to the Rescue 9

Boos for Roy 9

Happy New Year? 11

Where's the D? 11

Back on Track 12

Muller Takes the Lead 12

Skrudland Is Traded 13

LeClair Speaks Up 13

0 Goals = 1 Point 13

All-Star Team Player Patrick Roy 14

Sean Hill Steps In 15

The NHL's Best 15

Roy Goes Down 15

Demers Suffers Chest Pains 15

Holding Off Quebec 16

Saved in Overtime 16

38 Special 17

Bounced by the Bruins 17

A Disappointing Third 18

The Playoffs 19

Division Semifinals 19

The Adams Division Finals 20

The Wales Conference Finals 22

The Stanley Cup Finals 24

Illegal-Stick Rule 24

Profile: Patrick Roy 29

Montreal Canadiens Team Statistics 30

Key to Abbreviations 31

Glossary 32

Not Enough Offense

In 1992, the Montreal Canadiens finished first in the National Hockey League's (NHL's) Adams Division of the Prince of Wales Conference with a 41-28-11 record. (They won 41 games, lost 28, and tied 11.) They had the best defensive club, allowing just 207 goals all season. But their defensive style of play proved to be their downfall. It placed too much pressure on the shoulders of their superstar goaltender, Patrick Roy (pronounced WAH).

Eventually, the pressure was too much. Roy looked tired in the playoff series against their division rivals, the Boston Bruins. Though Roy had a Goals Against Average (GAA) of 2.62 in the playoffs, he allowed some questionable goals. The Canadiens' weak offense could not take up the slack. The Bruins bounced Montreal from the playoffs in a four-game sweep.

During the off-season, management took a hard look at their team. They knew they had good players. Besides Roy, the young but effective defense was anchored by two 23-year-old players—Eric Desjardins (day-jar-DANZ) and Mathieu Schneider. And the offense had its share of talented players such as veterans Denis Savard and Kirk Muller—the team's leading scorer in 1992. Even more, the addition of high-scoring Vincent Damphousse (dahm-FOOS) and Brian Bellows brought high hopes for a more potent offensive attack.

Since the core of the team was solid, management decided that a coaching change was in order. They wanted a coach who would put more emphasis on scoring. But Coach Pat Burns' disciplined defensive style was too slow.

The Montreal press often criticized Burns for his lack of offense, and he decided to leave the Canadiens to take the coaching job in Toronto. That left the door open for management to hire another coach. They decided to hire former Quebec, St. Louis, and Detroit coach Jacques Demers. Management hoped that Demers could maintain the high standards of defense necessary to win hockey championships, while getting more offense out of his talented offensive players. Despite the coaching change, most hockey experts picked Montreal to finish in the middle of the pack in the Adams Division for the 1992-93 season.

Vincent Damphousse added to the Canadiens offensive attack.

Slow Start

The Canadiens began the first week of the 1992-93 season with a 1-1-1 start. They lost Brian Skrudland in the opening seconds of the season against the Hartford Whalers when he suffered torn knee ligaments. Even more, Guy Carbonneau and Patrice Brisebois remained out with injuries.

WEEK 1 **1-1-1**

Still, Montreal fans saw some encouraging signs. Oleg Petrov looked fast and dangerous with his new line mates, Vincent Damphousse and Brian Bellows. Experts wondered if the Canadiens had dropped their defensive style.

"We haven't changed anything except we added that Damphousse line," said Demers. "All we're asking is our defense to get more involved in the offense—as long as they are disciplined."

When Brian Bellows played on the same line as Damphousse, the Canadiens had a new offensive style.

The Shake-Up

By the following week, the Canadiens were still struggling to make Coach Demers' offense work. They went 0-3-1 and were 1 for 35 on the power play. To shake the team up, Demers called his team to report at 6 a.m. for a 7 a.m. practice. During the very next game, the offense exploded in an 8-1 rout against the Minnesota North Stars.

WEEK 2 **2-3-1**

Despite the Canadiens 2-3-1 record, Pittsburgh Penguin superstar Mario Lemieux noticed some offensive improvement. "Montreal is playing a much different style and has some people like Brian Bellows and Vincent Damphousse to score," he said. "The problem is they've been playing defensively for 75 years, so the change is kind of tough."

Coach Demers of the Montreal Canadiens.

The Offense Kicks-In High Gear

A 5-3-2 record at the end of Week 3 signaled a turning point for the Canadiens. And no one turned around quicker than high-flying Denis Savard. Savard had successive three-point games against San Jose and the New York Rangers, and finished with 17 points in just nine games. Guy Carbonneau was back on the ice. It was no coincidence that the Canadiens went 4-0-1 with him in the lineup.

WEEK 3 5-3-2

But the biggest news was the offensive play of Todd Ewen. Known as a brawler, Ewen had never scored more than four goals in any of his first six NHL seasons. But in Week 3, Ewen had four goals in a three-game span. He scored two goals against his ex-teammates in a 6-2 victory over the St. Louis Blues. Then he scored a goal in an 8-4 rout of San Jose, and finished off with another goal in a 3-3 tie against the New York Rangers.

Overall, the offensive output pleased Canadien fans. And it looked as though Demers' system was going to pay off for the rest of the season.

Streaking Along

The Canadiens were the hottest team in the NHL after Week 4. They extended their unbeaten streak to 6-0-1 after defeating the New York Rangers. Defenseman Lyle Odelein had the NHL's best plus-minus rating (plus-13) through October. And newcomer Brian Bellows scored his ninth goal in 12 games in a 4-3 victory over the Rangers.

WEEK 4 7-3-2

Sweet Revenge

The streak continued (9-0-1) the following week, including two victories over the Detroit Red Wings (4-3 in Detroit, 5-1 in Montreal). During the streak, the Canadiens had outscored their opponents 51-27. At the Forum, their home arena, Montreal was 7-0-1 where they had outscored their opponents 41-18.

WEEK 5 10-3-3

The victories over Detroit were especially sweet for Coach Demers. Demers had been fired from Detroit even though he had won Coach of the Year awards two years in a row.

Savvy Savard

In Week 6, the Philadelphia Flyers ended Montreal's 12-game unbeaten streak—the NHL's longest since the Calgary Flames went 13 games without a loss in 1988-89. It was also the first loss for the Canadiens at the Forum after an 8-0-1 start.

WEEK 6 12-4-2

Even though Montreal was off to such a great start, they were one point behind last season's pace. In 1991, the Canadiens started the season at 13-4-1 and had scored 64 goals while giving up 27. After 18 games in the 1992-93 season, the Canadiens had scored 82 goals while giving up 58.

Denis Savard shows a lot of hustle.

"We were used to a style of laying back last year, playing strong D [defense]," said defenseman Mathieu Schneider. "But the guys are a lot more happy, getting more involved."

No one was happier than Denis Savard. He and his teammates, Stephan Lebeau (leh-BOW) and Kirk Muller, were in the top 25 in scoring. And all three played on different lines.

"Savvy (Savard) has been playing great," said Schneider. "The looser atmosphere has helped him."

Savard agreed. "We had some problems in the locker room last year," he said. That was then, this is now.

The Comeback Kids

It was clear after a 3-1 record in Week 7 that the Canadiens were no fluke, and that they would remain one of the top teams in the NHL. They were playing as a team. And each week, more and more players contributed to their success.

Coach Demers praised two of his young defensemen, Mathieu Schneider and Eric Desjardins. "Schneider is playing like a Norris winner," he said.

WEEK
7
15-5-2

(The Norris Trophy goes to the NHL's top defenseman. For more information, see the book *The Year in Sports 1993—Hockey's Heroes*.) "And Desjardins is looking like a general out there."

The Norris Trophy is awarded to the NHL's top defenseman.

The Canadiens had been enjoying their success without Guy Carbonneau who was out with a broken finger. And their offensive punch did not suffer. Even though they fell behind 3-0 to Boston and 2-0 to Ottawa, they bounced back for victories.

"We have put ourselves in the hole an awful lot lately and then dig ourselves out," Schneider said. "We can't keep doing that." The Canadiens needed better goaltending from Patrick Roy, who was having an average season.

Skrudland Skates

The Canadiens got encouraging news in Week 8. Brian Skrudland resumed skating and planned to return to the lineup for Montreal's four-game road trip to Boston, Winnipeg, Chicago, and Los Angeles. Critics called him "brittle" because he had missed 106 games in four seasons because of injuries. Skrudland did not like that nickname.

WEEK
8
16-6-3

"Brittle is candy," he said. "The last few years, I'm the guy who keeps taking a licking. Injuries are part of the game. Unfortunately, they're more part of my game than others."

Coach Demers said he would find a spot for Skrudland because he was so competitive. But he also admitted it might be a while before Skrudland returned to his center position.

Demers was also concerned about Patrick Roy. He did not want to tire him out for the playoffs. Roy had played an amazing 67 games last year. Through the first 25 games of the current season, Roy played 19 times for an 11-

Backup goalie Andre Racicot showed much improvement during the year.

5-3 record. Demers admitted he would use backup goalie Andre Racicot, who was 5-1—including a 6-1 victory over the Hartford Whalers in Week 8.

An Offensive Defense

The Canadiens continued their winning ways the following week. And the growing concerns about Vincent Damphousse had eased.

Before the season began, the Canadiens had given up Brent Gilchrist, Shayne Corson, and Vladimir Vujtek to Edmonton to get Damphousse for his scoring ability. But through November 20, Damphousse had only four goals. Demers even pulled him from a line with Muller and Bellows in favor of John LeClair. Still, Damphousse did not seem to be worried.

WEEK 9 18-7-3

"I have been through this before," he said. "Last year, I didn't do a thing for about 15 games. Then I scored a bunch. If I'm patient, things will change."

His patience paid off. Damphousse scored his 11th goal of the season in overtime to lift the Canadiens over the Winnipeg Jets in Week 9.

Even the defense was pitching in. They had scored 32 goals last season. Through Week 9, the Montreal defense had already dented the net for 28 goals. But they were still playing good defense. For the season, the Canadiens had taken 13 leads into the third period. They had yet to lose one.

Damphousse Arrives

After getting only three points on their road trip through Boston, Chicago, Winnipeg, and Los Angeles, the Canadiens returned home for a 5-1 victory over the Boston Bruins. Roy was the goaltender in three of the four road games, and was scheduled to play another three-of-four against Boston, the New York Rangers, and back-to-back games against Quebec. Racicot was the netminder against Winnipeg and played well. It looked as though he would become the top-notch backup goaltender Montreal so desperately needed.

WEEK 10
19-8-4

Meanwhile Vincent Damphousse's scoring drought was over. In a few short weeks, he had gone from a struggling player to the Canadiens' top scorer. Damphousse notched his second hat trick of the season against the Los Angeles Kings in the first-ever NHL game played in Phoenix. In dramatic fashion, Damphousse led a furious rally with three goals in a 7:09 span. He scored at 12:20, 17:06, and 19:29 of the third period, lifting Montreal to a 5-5 tie.

The Veterans to the Rescue

Week 11 did not start well for Montreal. They were bombed 10-5 by Boston, then fell 5-1 to Quebec. It looked like the beginning of a losing streak. But then the veteran players—like Skrudland, Savard, and Carbonneau—stepped up and helped rally the Canadiens. Montreal won 8-3 in Quebec—the second game of the back-to-back series. Then the Canadiens returned home to whip the Buffalo Sabres. The victory kept the Canadiens in first place in the Adams Division.

WEEK 11
21-10-4

"We have veterans like Brian Skrudland, Denis Savard, and Guy Carbonneau who don't accept losing," said Coach Demers. "It was important that no one panicked. The players didn't panic. The organization didn't. Even the fans and media didn't panic. It gave us a chance to regroup and go win."

Boos for Roy

Christmas week was no gift for the Canadiens as they bickered—and lost. Demers wanted to play Andre Racicot against the Whalers on December 21. But Patrick Roy insisted that he play. Demers gave in.

"It was Patrick's request and I respect that as a coach," he said. "I'm flexible." But Roy allowed three goals in the first 3:33 of the third period in a 5-2 loss against Hartford. The fans booed Roy for his performance.

WEEK 12
21-12-4

Two days later, Roy started a game at home against the New York Islanders. He was pulled early in the second period after Montreal fell behind 4-1. The Canadiens eventually lost 6-2. Afterward, the press criticized Demers for using Roy. Demers was not happy with the comments.

"I can't have people telling me how to coach," he snapped. "If it doesn't work, I'll pay the price."

Brian Skrudland has been a very
effective checker. He is quick, strong,
and a very hard worker.

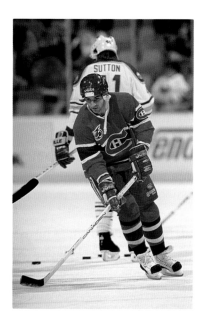

Denis Savard's strength is in his speed
and quickness. He jumps in and out of
openings and uses open ice just about
as well as any player in the game.

Guy Carbonneau has a small but wiry
frame and is deceptively strong. He is
tireless and doesn't quit in pursuit of a
bouncing puck in front of the net or in
pursuit of a puck carrier.

On the upside, Lyle Odelein's plus-27 rating was two behind league leader Mario Lemieux. Mike Keane had a plus-24 rating and was in a four-way tie for fourth.

Happy New Year?

Early in the season, the Canadiens could not lose at home. But as 1993 emerged, Montreal could not win at home or on the road. Even worse, the once-lowly Quebec Nordiques were in first place!

WEEK **13** 22-14-5

Montreal lost to Hartford and the Islanders at the Forum. Then they went on a road trip where they lost in Vancouver and Calgary. Their only victory came in Edmonton against the Oilers.

During the losing streak, the Canadiens played a different, conservative style. They blew a 2-0 lead in Calgary. Then they spotted Edmonton two goals on the Oilers' first two shots before storming back to win. "We've lacked killer instinct," Schneider admitted.

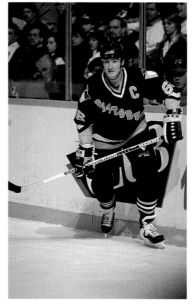

Mario Lemieux of the Pittsburgh Penguins.

Where's the D?

The Canadiens had won the Jennings Trophy for the least number of goals allowed in the league four of the last six seasons. But as they passed the midway point of the 1992-93 season, they were fifth in goals allowed—30 behind the league-leading Chicago Blackhawks.

Canadien fans knew that the defense would suffer since Demers opened up the style of play to create more goals. But Montreal had been playing below .500 (losing more than winning) the past three weeks. Patrick Roy needed a 2-1 victory in San Jose to snap a five-game winless streak.

WEEK **14** 24-15-5

"Patrick's confidence has been shaky," Mathieu Schneider said. "We needed to play well in front of him."

Despite his shaky confidence, Roy was named as the starting goalie for the All-Star Game after winning the fan balloting.

Also during Week 14, former Canadien coach Pat Burns returned to the Forum with his revived Toronto Maple Leafs. Toronto won 5-4. Denis Savard missed his third game with a mild right-knee sprain.

Back on Track

After a 2-6-1 stretch, the Canadiens were back on track. They won five of six games, including two victories each over Hartford and San Jose, and one victory over Quebec. Their only loss came at the Forum at the hands of the Toronto Maple Leafs.

WEEK 15
28-15-5

Stephan Lebeau (leh-BOW) and Vincent Damphousse led the way with nine points each in four games. Lebeau surpassed his career-best 58-points. And Andre Racicot played consecutive games for the first time all season.

Patrick Roy had this to say about the slump: "It's normal to have a slump in the middle of the season. We're just going to have to keep on pushing hard to find a way out of it."

Muller Takes the Lead

The Canadiens' rebound was slowed in Week 16 when they were shelled at New Jersey (6-2) and Toronto (4-0). The loss against the Devils snapped Montreal's five-game winning streak. Two nights earlier, the Canadiens defeated the Devils 3-2 at the Forum. Former New Jersey winger Kirk Muller scored the winning goal and his

WEEK 16
29-17-5

team-leading 63rd point. Benoit Brunet went out indefinitely with a broken thumb when he was slashed by New Jersey's John MacLean.

"You get a slash one game, and you're not going to try to hurt your team that game," said Brian Skrudland. "But you're going to take down the license number and get your whack the next 60 minutes."

Rumors were circulating that Skrudland, Carbonneau, and Savard were on the trading block because of their inconsistent play.

Stephan Lebeau has every offensive tool needed in hockey except size. Lebeau has great hockey sense. He can score with a quick-release wrist shot, or make a good pass. Lebeau needs to work with players who will get him the puck.

Skrudland Is Traded

It took only one week before the rumor became fact. After eight years with the Montreal Canadiens, Brian Skrudland was traded to Calgary for Gary Leeman.

Skrudland ended his career in Montreal on January 27 when he took a game misconduct penalty for spearing in a 6-5 loss to the Whalers. In 23 games during the 1992-93 season, Skrudland had five goals and eight points. "It's been a great eight years," he said after the trade was announced.

Canadien General Manager Serge Savard hoped Leeman would contribute. "I'm not saying he will score 50 goals for us," he said, "but all we want is some goals. Skrudland's role had diminished."

Ed Ronan, a checker who often replaced Skrudland on the ice, scored an overtime goal to beat the Bruins in Week 17.

LeClair Speaks Up

Winger John LeClair scored a goal and two points in a 7-2 victory over Los Angeles as the Canadiens went 2-0 in Week 18. After the game, LeClair stated confidently that he could contribute even more.

"I believe I can play like that every night," he said. "It's the way the club wants me to play. But what I've got to do is play consistently. With injuries and with the little time I've played, I don't think I've played more than a game and a half the last three weeks. That makes things tough."

While LeClair hoped to emerge as a player, Lyle Odelein saw his play slip. Since Mathieu Schneider went down with a sprained ankle, Odelein's plus-minus rating dropped from plus-30 to plus-26.

0 Goals = 1 Point

Coming off the All-Star break in February, the Canadiens went 2-0-1 on a road trip. One game included a 0-0 tie with the Philadelphia Flyers—the first 0-0 tie since the Rangers and the Islanders did it on December 9, 1989.

The Canadiens were in first place—and that's where they wanted to stay. "Our goal right now is to finish first in the Adams Division and first overall," Demers said. "But we have to remember that the playoffs, the Stanley Cup, is the most important goal."

All-Star Team Player
Patrick Roy

In 1993, Patrick Roy was one of the top goalies in the NHL. In 1992, he won the Vezina Trophy as the league's best goaltender.

At the All-Star Break						
	GP	AVG.	W	L	T	SO
Patrick Roy, Montreal	41	3.12	21	15	5	2
Final Season Statistics						
Montreal Goalies	GP	AVG.	W	L	T	SO
Patrick Roy	62	3.2	31	25	5	2
Frederic Chabot	1	1.5	0	0	0	0
Andre Racicot	26	3.39	17	5	1	1

Sean Hill Steps In

In a 1-1 week, Denis Savard separated his shoulder and was expected to miss as much as three weeks. Savard added his name to the growing list of injured: Gary Leeman, Guy Carbonneau, Benoit Brunet, Mike Keane, and Mathieu Schneider. Because of the injuries, Demers turned to defenseman Sean Hill for help. Hill, a U.S. Olympian, hoped he could play full-time.

WEEK
20
36-19-6

"He hasn't accepted the idea of not playing," said Demers. "I like that."

The NHL's Best

WEEK
21
40-19-6

Week 21 was one of the Canadiens' best. By the end of the week, they had won five in a row and were on a 10-1-1 streak that vaulted them to the top of the overall standings—four points better than Pittsburgh. Montreal became the first NHL team to earn a playoff berth when they thrashed the Buffalo Sabres 8-4.

Todd Ewen returned to the lineup, but Guy Carbonneau, Donald Dufresne, Matt Schneider, Benoit Brunet, and Denis Savard were still out. Gary Leeman's consistent play was making it even harder for them to return to the lineup.

Brian Bellows notched his first four-goal game with the Canadiens in a victory over Buffalo. It was also the third of his career.

Roy Goes Down

After enjoying so much success, Week 22 put the brakes on Montreal's climb to the top of the NHL's heap. All-Star goalie Patrick Roy left the game in Minnesota with a strained hip flexor muscle. He was expected to miss 7 to 10 days. Earlier in the week, he had played brilliantly in a win against Boston. But then the Canadiens dropped a game to lowly Tampa before losing to Minnesota.

WEEK
22
41-21-6

Jesse Belanger scored his first two NHL goals against the North Stars. Winger Mike Keane took the plus-minus lead with a plus-36 rating. Defenseman Lyle Odelein was second with a plus-35 mark.

Demers Suffers Chest Pains

WEEK
23
42-23-6

Demers hoped the following week would get better for his Canadiens— but it didn't. They finished 1-2-0—including a 5-2 loss to the Nordiques at the Forum—and saw their first-place lead over Quebec slip to a mere four points. Kirk Muller joined the crowded injured list with a sprained wrist.

Even worse, Demers checked himself into the hospital on March 9 after suffering chest pains. He was released a few days later with a clean bill of health. A nutritionist told him to lose 25 pounds—and learn to relax.

"This scared the heck out of me," he said. "I thought I was having a heart attack. All the pressure I put on myself, I'm the one who does it. They say I eat my emotions. I believe that. I could have six or seven pieces of pizza and then go out to dinner with my wife and not even really remember the pizza."

While he was in the hospital, the Canadiens rallied for a 5-1 victory over the New York Islanders. Assistant General Manager Jacques Lemaire guided the Canadiens to the victory. (He last coached the Canadiens in 1984-85.)

Holding Off Quebec

The Canadiens got a much-needed victory at Quebec in Week 24. They had lost four-of-five games before the win. But John LeClair had his 10-point scoring streak snapped at Quebec.

WEEK 24
44-23-6

Left winger Gilbert Dionne was the key player in the victory as the Canadiens went 3 for 4 on the power play. Montreal also held the Nordiques to 0 for 6 on their power plays.

With Boston surging toward first place in the Adams Division, it looked as though Montreal and Quebec might meet in the playoffs. Both clubs were 3-3 against each other—the visiting team winning each time.

A very determined player, Muller has limited skills, but makes up for it with hard work. He is not a great open ice skater. But his balance and strength in traffic make him one of the best players to have on the ice in a last second scramble for a tying or winning goal.

Saved in Overtime

The following week, the Canadiens needed overtime victories over Hartford and Ottawa to avoid disaster. They lost 8-3 to Buffalo and 2-0 in Boston before rebounding with the overtime wins.

Despite their 2-2 finish for the week, Whalers Captain Pat Verbeek said the Canadiens were the best team in the Adams Division. "In the playoffs," he said, "you need balance. And I see Montreal with the best balance." Whaler Coach Paul Holmgren added: "From an experience standpoint, they've got an advantage."

WEEK 25
46-25-6

38 Special

Week 26 was another disappointment for the Canadiens. They dropped consecutive lopsided losses. Then in a game against the Islanders, Montreal was down 2-1 after two periods. But then Brian Bellows scored his 38th goal and Vincent Damphousse followed with his 38th for the dramatic 3-2 win.

WEEK
26
47-27-6

The victory kept the Canadiens two points ahead of the Nordiques and three ahead of the surging Boston Bruins. But Montreal had tough assignments ahead—home games against the Washington Capitals and Boston Bruins and road games at Buffalo and league-leading Pittsburgh.

Bounced by the Bruins

In a week when they needed to win, the Canadiens could not gain a point. The most costly defeat came at the hands of the Boston Bruins in Montreal, where the Canadiens lost 5-1. With the victory, the Bruins clinched the Adams Division title. It was part of their amazing 16-3 run since they were in third place and 15 points out of first on March 3.

Despite the loss to the Bruins, the Canadiens still had much to play for. A second place showdown with Quebec was at stake—and home ice advantage in the first round of the playoffs.

WEEK
27
47-29-6

Montreal had to face the hottest team in the NHL—the Pittsburgh Penguins. Pittsburgh had won 14 in a row—and were gunning for the record of 15 set by the 1982 New York Islanders.

The Canadiens played tough against the Penguins. They held superstar Mario Lemieux to only two assists, breaking his 11-game goal streak. But Ulf Samuelsson beat the Canadiens in overtime, 4-3.

"We kept the best player in the world in check," Demers said afterward. "But if he doesn't hurt you, someone else will."

Now the Canadiens were tied with Quebec for second place with 100 points each. And they would play each other in the playoffs for the first time since 1987. Only one questioned remained: Who would win second place and gain home ice advantage?

In Week 27, the Canadiens broke Mario Lemieux's 11-game goal streak.

A Disappointing Third

Montreal went 1-1 in the last week of the regular season. In the final game in Buffalo, Brian Bellows scored the game-tying goal late in the third period. Then he notched the game-winner in overtime to give the Canadiens a 3-2 victory.

Despite the win, the Canadiens finished in third place of the Adams Division, two points behind the second-place Quebec Nordiques. Quebec won their last two games, including a 6-2 win against the Ottawa Senators.

For the season, the Canadiens finished with 102 points—good for sixth overall in the NHL. Their 326 goals were ninth best.

Though Canadien fans were disappointed about the regular season finish, they were not worried about the playoffs. They were sure Montreal would regroup in time to bring home another Stanley Cup. And nothing less would do.

The Playoffs

Division Semifinals

The opening playoff round against the Quebec Nordiques had a special twist to it. Both the Canadiens and the Nordiques played in the Quebec Province of Canada, so both teams wanted to represent their region in the Stanley Cup Finals.

The Nordiques won the regular season series 4-3. But 18 of Quebec's 26 players—including five of their top six scorers—had never been in an NHL playoff game. Some experts thought the Canadiens would be knocked out in the first round for the first time since 1983. But Montreal's playoff experience would play a big part in the series. And then there was Patrick Roy, whom many thought was the game's best goaltender.

In the first game at Quebec, Montreal took a 2-0 lead late into the third period. Roy was sharp and the defense played flawlessly. Then disaster struck.

Quebec scored a power play goal at 18:31 of the third period. The score ignited the crowd—and the Nordiques. At 19:12, Quebec notched the game-tying goal—sending the game into overtime.

Montreal was in shock, and couldn't recover. Quebec's Scott Young scored at 16:49 to lift the Nordiques to a dramatic come-from-behind victory. It looked as though Quebec—not Montreal—was the team with the experience.

Game 2 belonged to Quebec. Montreal still looked stunned as the Nordiques scored three times in the first period, then held on for a 4-1 win. They led the Canadiens 2-0 in the best-of-seven series as the playoff shifted to the Forum in Montreal.

Canadien fans hoped that the home ice would help their team in Game 3. But Quebec scored the first and only goal of the first period for a 1-0 lead. Montreal came out smoking in the second period and scored the game-tying goal at 1:50. For the rest of the game, the Canadiens peppered Quebec goalie Ron Hextall with 38 shots. But the fiesty Hextall did not break as the game went into overtime. A goal by the Nordiques would be a disaster. It would put them up 3-0 in the series—a nearly insurmountable lead.

Hextall faced another barrage of shots in the overtime period. At 10:30, Hextall made his 48th save. But the rebound hit a teammate's skate and went into the net. Vincent Damphousse was credited with the game-winning goal. Quebec protested the score, but it was denied. Montreal had won an important game, and shaved Quebec's lead to 2-1.

Game 4 was another tightly-fought contest. But Montreal prevailed 3-2, tying the series at two games apiece. In Game 5 in Quebec, Montreal took a 1-0 lead after one period. But Quebec responded with three second-period goals and tied up the game going into the third period. Quebec took a 4-3 lead at 6:16 of the third period, but the Canadiens tied the score at 13:23. Roy made 14 saves in the third period and helped send the game into overtime.

Quebec sent five shots at Roy in overtime, and he turned aside each one. But the Canadiens had yet to get a shot on goal, and their chances did not look good. Finally, Kirk Muller took Vincent Damphousse's pass on his forehand and ripped a low shot that caught goalie Ron Hextall on the move at 8:17 of overtime. Montreal's only overtime shot produced the game-winning goal and a 5-4 victory. Now they had a 3-2 game lead—and could close out the series at Montreal.

Game 6 seemed like a close contest. After all, three of the five games went into overtime, and all five games were decided by one-goal margins. Ed Ronan scored the first goal of the game in the first period, and the Canadiens took a 4-2 lead into the third period. But Quebec could not mount a comeback. Paul Di Pietro and Dionne finished the scoring for Montreal as they won easily, 6-2.

Di Pietro had three goals and an assist as the Canadiens clinched their Adams Division semifinal series 4-2. Though Di Pietro was benched the last three games, he finished a 3-on-2 rush for his second goal to break a 2-2 tie in the second period.

Next up for the Canadiens was the Adams Division finals against the Buffalo Sabres who swept division champion Boston in 4 games.

The Adams Division Finals

Because Buffalo finished fourth in the division, Montreal earned the home ice advantage for the division finals. In Game 1, they made sure they did not waste the opportunity. Vincent Damphousse's goal 6:50 into the third period broke the game's final tie and gave the Montreal Canadiens a 4-3 victory and a 1-0 series lead.

Patrick Roy was the real star. He faced 35 shots and turned back 32, while the Canadiens could only muster 22 shots against Grant Fuhr. Luckily, the Canadiens made them count.

In Game 2, Guy Carbonneau scored 2:50 into overtime as the Canadiens won 4-3 for a 2-0 series lead. Ed Ronan won a race into the Buffalo zone and freed the puck for Denis Savard. Savard fed Carbonneau at the side of the net for the game-winner.

Patrick Roy was the real star in the first game of the Adams Division Finals. He turned back 32 of 35 shots to defeat Buffalo.

Vincent Damphousse had two goals for the Canadiens. Kirk Muller scored the other. Once again, Buffalo outshot the Canadiens 31-25. But Patrick Roy was hot again, and cooled off the Sabres. The series now shifted for Games 3 and 4 in Buffalo.

Sabre fans hoped the home ice would help their team in Game 3. But Montreal grabbed a quick 2-0 lead in the first period on goals by Muller and Damphousse.

Buffalo tied the score 2-2 after two periods, and the teams exchanged goals in the third period to send the contest into overtime.

Once again, the Sabres shelled the Canadien net—this time with 5 shots in overtime. Patrick Roy turned them all aside.

Eight minutes into the overtime period, Patrice Brisebois flipped the puck toward the Buffalo net just inside the blue line. Dionne redirected it past a stunned Grant Fuhr on Montreal's only shot in the extra period. Montreal won 4-3 and took a commanding 3-0 series lead. The victory was the Canadiens' second in a row in overtime and was the series' third consecutive 4-3 final. It was the record 18th overtime playoff game this season. Brian Bellows pitched in with two assists. Now the Canadiens were one victory away from the Wales Conference Finals.

In Game 4, Buffalo put up another tough fight. But at the end of three periods, they found themselves in a familiar 3-3 tie going into overtime. They hoped the trend would not continue—but it did. Kirk Muller notched the game-winner for Montreal, giving the

The
Playoffs
BUFFALO

Canadiens a 4-0 series sweep and a berth into the Conference finals against the surprising New York Islanders. The Islanders had defeated the defending Stanley Cup Champion Pittsburgh Penguins in dramatic fashion—a Game 7 overtime win. They would prove to be a tough challenge.

The Wales Conference Finals

The Canadiens had more than a week to rest up for the Islanders. Defenseman Mathieu Schneider was able to recover from a separated shoulder. And Brian Bellows was able to nurse cracked ribs. But the Canadiens also worried about being rusty.

"At first, it was nice to have time off," said John LeClair. "But as the week went on, it got old. We were anxious to play."

After the eight-day layoff, Montreal came out sizzling in Game 1 of the Wales Conference finals. John LeClair had his first two goals of the playoffs to spark the Canadiens' offense. They took a 3-0 lead into the final period and never looked back as they held the Islanders to just 11 shots in the first 40 minutes. The two teams exchanged goals in the final period as the Canadiens went on to an easy 4-1 win and a 1-0 series lead. With the win, the Canadiens tied a team record for consecutive playoff wins (nine). Patrick Roy became the fifth NHL goaltender with 60 or more career playoff wins.

"I thought the adrenaline would be up more than it was," said Islander goaltender Glenn Healy. "We have to readjust. Montreal is a much tighter-checking team than Pittsburgh."

"We had to be well-prepared to play against the team that shocked the hockey world two days ago," said Demers. Well-prepared they were.

In Game 2, Montreal pushed their playoff winning streak to a club-record 10 games. But it took another overtime victory to do it. Stephan Lebeau took a pass from Vincent Damphousse and drilled a slap shot high over the glove of goalie Glenn Healy at 6:21 of the second overtime for a 4-3 victory. The goal was his second of the game and the playoffs. With the win, Montreal took a 2-0 series lead into New York for Game 3.

"I didn't have a lot of success so far offensively," Lebeau said afterward. "But maybe things turned around tonight. I was patient, I was playing well defensively, and I made sacrifices offensively."

In Game 3, the Montreal Canadiens' playoff winning streak hit a record-tying 11 games with a 2-1 overtime win. Guy Carbonneau took Benoit Brunet's pass and scored from the left faceoff circle at 12:34. It was Montreal's seventh overtime win this season, breaking the Islanders 1980 record.

"In overtime, we just tell the guys to go for it," said Coach Demers. "That's the kind of confidence we have now."

The Canadiens forced the game into overtime when Vincent Damphousse scored at 14:46 of the third period. That wiped out a 1-0 lead Pierre Turgeon gave New York at 1:36 of the second period.

Coach Demers prepared his team well for the battle against the New York Islanders in the Wales Conference Finals.

"We weren't worried because of our success in overtime the last month or so," said Paul Di Pietro. "We stayed patient and worked hard and then we capitalized on our chance. We were pretty confident out there."

Patrick Roy was outstanding in goal, turning away 31 of 32 Islander shots—including four in the overtime period.

The Islanders saved face in Game 4 with a solid 4-1 victory. But the series returned to Montreal for its eventual outcome. The Canadiens reached the Stanley Cup finals for the 34th time in 83 years with a 5-2 win.

"The boys had a little fun carrying around the Wales Conference trophy," said Brian Bellows, who had a goal and two assists. "But it wasn't overdone. We know what it takes to go the final step."

"In my first year as Canadiens coach, this is gratifying," said Demers. "The most important thing for me is not to let anyone down."

Before the final game, Demers came up with an idea to give his team the boost it needed to advance to the finals. Demers inserted Mike Keane at right wing with Kirk Muller and John LeClair. The LeClair-Muller-Keane line opened up a 2-0 lead after one period on Muller's first goal of the series and Keane's second in the playoffs. Muller's goal, set up by Keane, came 58 seconds into the game.

"I put Keane with Muller because I thought the Islanders were doing a good job checking Muller," Demers said. "I thought Mike would open it up a little bit."

Brian Bellows left the Muller line to join Damphousse and Lebeau. That line triggered a second-period blitz that built a 5-0 Canadien lead.

"The way the guys were fired up in the dressing room, you could have put our substitute goaltender at center to start the game," Bellows said.

Though Guy Carbonneau was held scoreless, he was a key player in the final game. During a penalty-killing shift, Carbonneau blocked two shots—after he had lost his stick.

After the victory, Montreal had to wait for the outcome of the Toronto/Los Angeles series. The Los Angeles Kings eventually won, setting the stage for a showdown with the legendary Wayne Gretzky.

The Stanley Cup Finals

The Stanley Cup Finals matched two third-place teams. The Canadiens had won the season series from the Kings 1-0-2. Though Montreal had more time to rest, experts picked the Kings to win the Cup. They liked Wayne Gretzky's Stanley Cup experience—and the fact that he was playing well. (In Game 7 against Toronto, he had scored a hat trick.) And overall, the Kings scored 12 more goals than the Canadiens in the regular season. They had high-scoring defenseman Alexi Zhitnik, toughman Marty McSorely, and team speed that could cause many problems defensively. If Montreal was going to win their record 24th Stanley Cup, they had to play tough defense.

In Game 1 in Montreal, the Kings served notice that they would be the Canadiens' toughest playoff foe. Luc Robitaille (ROW-bih-tie) scored two goals as the Kings cruised to an easy 4-1 victory and a 1-0 series lead. Wayne Gretzky also had a goal and three assists.

"Gretzky toyed with us tonight," Demers said afterward.

Meanwhile, Tony Granato and linemates Mike Donnelly and Corey Millen caused major problems for the Montreal defense, who could not handle their speed.

Despite the loss, Roy played well. He turned aside 19 of 20 shots in the second period alone, and finished the game with 34 saves. But the Canadiens weren't sharp, and they needed to play better before the Kings skated away with the Cup.

Game 2 was a different story. But the result was strangely familiar for the Canadiens. Defenseman Eric Desjardins completed his hat trick 51 seconds into overtime as Montreal won 3-2 to even the series at 1-1. Desjardins scored with 1:13 left in regulation to tie the game after the Kings were assessed a two-minute penalty because defenseman Marty McSorely used an illegal stick. The Kings did not argue the call.

"When a stick is like his," Wayne Gretzky said afterward, "it's pretty obvious. Marty has a big curve. It's easy to see."

Referee Kerry Fraser measured the curvature of McSorely's stick at the request of the Canadiens' bench. Then Coach Demers pulled goaltender Patrick Roy to add a sixth attacker. Desjardins took advantage of the situation to beat Los Angeles goalie Kelly·

Illegal-Stick Rule

Rule 20B of the NHL rule book says the blade of the stick shall not be more than 3 inches (7.5 centimeters) in width at any point, nor less than 2 inches (5 centimeters). The curvature of the blade shall be restricted to a maximum of one-half inch (1.25 centimeters).

The Canadiens would have been assessed a bench minor for delay of game if they had been wrong about McSorely's stick. But they weren't. And because of it, they won the game.

The STANLEY CUP Finals

Wayne Gretzky's elegant skating is terrifying to his defenders. Gretzky has incredible puck control and his backhand shot allows him to protect the puck with his body.

Hrudey with a long slap shot. Montreal forward John LeClair screened Hrudey, who had 38 saves in the game.

After the game, Bryan Lewis, the NHL's supervisor of officials, showed that McSorely's stick was "at least a quarter inch" beyond the maximum allowed.

The finals went west for the first time in its 100-year history as Game 3 was played at the Forum in Los Angeles. Brian Bellows opened the scoring at 10:26 of the first period. Dionne made it 2-0 at 2:41 of the second period. Then at 3:02, Schneider made it 3-0 in favor of the Canadiens. With Patrick Roy in goal, the lead seemed insurmountable.

But the Kings had Wayne Gretzky on the ice, and no lead was safe. Gretzky controlled a pass behind the Canadien net, toyed with Montreal's defense, then found Luc Robitaille out front with a perfect pass. Robitaille snapped a shot past Roy—and the comeback began.

Tony Granato brought the Kings within 3-2 with an unassisted goal. He intercepted a pass in the Montreal zone and drove a shot between Roy's legs. Then Gretzky took a pass at full speed outside the Canadien blue line. He skated to the top of the left circle and drove a shot over Roy's glove. The puck found the net and—in less than 11 minutes—the game was tied at 3-3.

In Game 5, Kirk Muller's 10th goal of the playoffs gave the Canadiens a 2-1 lead.

The third period went scoreless, forcing yet another overtime session. LeClair ended it quickly, swatting in a rebound past Kings' goalie Kelly Hrudey at 34 seconds.

"It's an unbelievable situation, what's happening to us right now in overtime," said Demers.

"Everybody was real confident in the locker room before the overtime," said LeClair. "We realize we've had success in overtime. Being tied 3-3 after three periods on the road, we liked that situation."

It also helped to have Patrick Roy in the net. Roy had not allowed an overtime goal since the Canadiens' first playoff game against Quebec.

"It's so important to have a goaltender of his caliber in the playoffs," said Carbonneau of Roy. "He was a little mad at himself after giving up those three goals in the second period. But he said, 'I'll be back in the third,' and we knew he would be."

The Canadiens needed just two more victories for their first Stanley Cup title since 1986.

Game 4 looked like a copy of Game 3. The Canadiens scored the only goal of the first period, then added to their lead with a goal by Damphousse at 5:24 of the second period. The Kings, however, mounted their comeback. They tied the game at 19:55 of the second period. A scoreless third period sent the game into overtime for the third game in a row.

The STANLEY CUP Finals

This time, however, the Kings would not go without a fight. They fired 10 shots at Roy in the extra period. But once again, he turned away every one. Finally, LeClair ended the suspense with an unassisted goal at 14:37. LeClair fired the puck at Hrudey on a 2-on-1 rush. Hrudey came out of the net to block the shot. The rebound bounced along the left goal line. LeClair's momentum carried him to the puck, and he slid it past Hrudey and off the arm of Kings defenseman Daryl Sydor, who tried to stop the goal.

"We won 10 straight overtime games for two reasons," Bellows said afterward. "Patrick Roy and we play 20 players. And nobody panics. You watch guys and there's no anxiety, none at all."

The Kings now had to win three consecutive games—two in Montreal—to win their first Stanley Cup. The Canadiens only had to win one.

There was no suspense in Game 5 at Montreal. The Kings and the Canadiens seemed to know the outcome before the opening faceoff. Montreal opened the scoring at 15:10 of the first period on a goal by Di Pietro. Kings defenseman Marty McSorely banged a shot off both posts and into the Canadien net at 2:40 of the second period to tie the score. But then Kirk Muller's 10th goal of the playoffs gave the Canadiens a 2-1 lead at 3:51. Stephan Lebeau's power-play goal, set up by a drop pass by Mike Keane, gave the Canadiens a two-goal lead at 11:31. When Di Pietro scored his second goal with 7:54 left in regulation, he danced on the toes of his skates for half of the ice before pumping his arms in a victory signal.

LeClair is a physical winger who makes good use of his size and strong skating. He scored the tie-breaking goal to win Game 4 of the Stanley Cup Finals.

The Canadiens hadn't clinched a Stanley Cup at the Montreal Forum since 1979, when they downed the New York Rangers in five games. National Hockey League holder Montreal has almost twice as many Cup titles (24) as the second-place Toronto Maple Leafs, whose 13th Cup title came in 1967.

Goaltender Patrick Roy, the playoff Most Valuable Player (MVP) in 1986 when he was a rookie, was named the winner of the Conn Smythe Trophy. He made 18 saves to earn his 16th playoff victory—12 coming by one goal and 10 in overtime. He also became the first Canadien to win the trophy twice.

Now that they have the Cup again, the Canadiens face an old challenge— one they haven't faced since 1986. They must defend Lord Stanley's Cup.

Profile

Patrick Roy

Years of NHL service: 7
Born: Quebec City, Que.; Oct. 5, 1965
Position: Goaltender
Height: 6-0
Weight: 175
Uniform no.: 33
Catches: Left
Highest achievement: MVP of the
     Stanley Cup Finals

Goaltender Patrick Roy was the MVP of the Stanley Cup Finals.

Montreal Canadiens
Team Statistics

Player	Gp	G	A	Pts	+/-	Pim	Pp
Damphousse	84	39	58	97	5	98	9
Muller	80	37	57	94	8	77	12
Bellows	82	40	48	88	4	44	16
Lebeau	71	31	49	80	23	20	8
Keane	77	15	45	60	29	95	0
Savard	63	16	34	50	1	90	4
Dionne	75	20	28	48	5	63	6
Desjardins	82	13	32	45	20	98	7
LeClair	72	19	25	44	11	33	2
Schneider	60	13	31	44	8	91	3
Leeman	50	15	17	32	14	24	1
Brisebois	70	10	21	31	6	79	4
Haller	73	11	14	25	7	117	6
Brunet	47	10	15	25	13	19	0
Daigneault	66	8	10	18	25	57	0
Ramage	74	5	13	18	-24	146	5
Di Pietro	29	4	13	17	11	14	0
Carbonneau	61	4	13	17	-9	20	0
Odelein	83	2	14	16	35	205	0
Ewen	75	5	9	14	6	193	0
Ronan	53	5	7	12	6	20	0
Roberge	50	4	4	8	2	142	0
Hill	31	2	6	8	-5	54	1
Dufresne	32	1	2	3	0	32	0

The Montreal Canadiens, 1993 Stanley Cup Champions.

Key to Abbreviations

A	Assists
Avg.	Goals-Against Average
G	Goals
GA	Goals Against
GP	Games Played
L	Losses
MP	Minutes Played
Pts.	Points
SA	Saves
W	Wins
PIM	Penalty Minutes
Pp.	Power Play Goals
+/-	Plus/Minus Rating—When a goal is scored, all players on the ice for the goal-scoring team receive 1 point. When a goal is scored against a team, all its players on the ice lose a point.

Glossary

Assist—A pass of the puck to the teammate scoring a goal.

Attacking zone—The part of the rink farthest from the defended goal.

Blue line—The parallel line 60 feet out from each goal line that extends completely across the rink.

Center—An offensive player who is positioned between the left and right wing players.

Center line—The red line that divides the rink in half.

Check—To slow or stop an opponent in control of the puck, either by blocking the player's progress with the body or by jabbing at the puck with the stick.

Defending zone—The part of the rink in which the goals are located.

Face off—To start play by releasing the puck between two opposing players.

Goal—The area into which players try to advance the puck; the score for such an act.

Goal crease—The area in front of each goal marked by a semicircular red line.

Goal line—The red line between the goal posts on the ice and extended completely across the rink.

Goal post—One of a pair of posts joined with a crossbar and set at each end of the hockey rink.

Goaltender—A player assigned to protect the goal.

Hat trick—When a player scores three goals in one game.

Neutral zone—The central part of the rink.

Penalty—A punishment or loss of advantage imposed on a team or competitor for violation of a rule.

Penalty box—Benches or seats located directly across from the players' benches where penalized players must remain until their penalty time has expired.

Rink—An area surfaced with smooth ice for hockey. The official size of the rink is 200 feet long and 85 feet wide.

Wing—Either of the forward positions played near the sidelines.